About this book

The First Thousand Words in Italian is an enormously popular book that has helped many thousands of children and adults learn new words and improve their Italian language skills.

You'll find it easy to learn words by looking at the **small labelled pictures**. Then you can practise the words by talking about the large central pictures. You can also **listen to the words** on the Usborne website (see below).

There is an alphabetical **word list** at the back of the book, which you can use to look up words in the picture pages.

Remember, this is a book of a thousand words. It will take time to learn them all.

Masculine and feminine words
When you look at Italian words for things such as "chair" or "man", you will see that they have **il, lo, la** or **l'** in front of them. This is because all Italian words for people and things are either masculine or feminine. **Il** or **lo** are the words for "the" in front of a masculine word, **la** is "the" in front of a feminine word, and you use **l'** in front of words that begin with "a", "e", "i", "o" or "u". For plurals (more than one, as in "chair" or "men"), the Italian word for "the" is **i** or **gli** for masculine words, and **le** for feminine words.

All the labels in this book show words for things with **il, lo, la, i, gli** or **le**. Always learn them with this little word.

Looking at Italian words
A few Italian words have an accent on the last letter of the word. This is a sign written over the letter, and means that the last part of the word is stressed when it is spoken.

How to say the Italian words
The best way to learn how to pronounce Italian words is to listen to a native Italian speaker. You can hear the words in this book, read by a native speaker, on the Usborne Quicklinks website. Just go to **www.usborne.com/quicklinks** and enter the keywords **1000 italian**. There you can also find links to other useful websites about Italy and the Italian language.

Please note that Usborne Publishing is not responsible for the content of external websites. Please follow the internet safety guidelines on the Usborne Quicklinks website.

i colori

le bottiglie

i pesci rossi

l'elicottero

il puzzle

la cioccolata

A casa

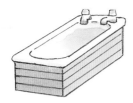

la vasca

il sapone

il rubinetto

la carta igienica

lo spazzolino

l'acqua

il gabinetto

la spugna

il lavandino

la doccia

l'asciugamano

il letto

Il bagno

Il soggiorno

il dentifricio

la radio

il cuscino

il DVD

la moquette

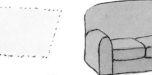

il divano

THE USBORNE
FIRST THOUSAND WORDS
IN ITALIAN

Heather Amery

Illustrated by Stephen Cartwright

Revised edition by Mairi Mackinnon
Picture editing by Mike Olley
Italian language consultant: Emanuela Guastella

There is a little yellow duck to look for on every
double page with pictures. Can you find it?

Stephen Cartwright's
little yellow duck made
his first-ever appearance in *The First
Thousand Words* over thirty years ago.
Duck has since featured in over 125
titles, in more than 70 languages, and
has delighted millions of readers,
both young and old,
around the world.

la sedia

 il piumone

il pettine

il lenzuolo

il tappeto

 l'armadio

La camera da letto

 il televisore

 il cassettone

 lo specchio

 la spazzola

 la lampada

L'ingresso

 i poster

 l'attaccapanni

 il telefono

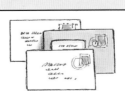 le scale

 il radiatore

la frutta

 il giornale

 il tavolino

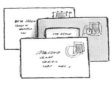 le lettere

5

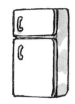

il frigorifero

i bicchieri

l'orologio

lo sgabello

i cucchiaini

l'interruttore

il detersivo

la chiave

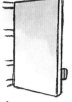

la porta

l'aspira-polvere

La cucina

il lavello

le pentole

le forchette

il grembiule

l'asse da stiro

la spazzatura

bollitore

 i coltelli

lo spazzolone

 lo straccio

 le mattonelle

la scopa

 la lavatrice

 la paletta

 il cassetto

 i piattini

 la padella

 la cucina

 i mestoli

 i piatti

 il ferro da stiro

 l'armadietto

 lo strofinaccio

 le tazze

 i fiammiferi

 la spazzola

 le scodelle

7

la carriola

l'alveare

la chiocciola

i mattoni

il piccione

la vanga

la coccinella

la pattumiera

i semi

il casotto

Il giardino

l'annaffiatoio

il verme

i fiori

l'annaffiatore

la zappa

la vespa

l'ape

la paletta

l'osso

la siepe

il forcone

il tosaerba

il sentiero

le foglie

l'albero

il fumo

il bruco

il rastrello

il nido

i ramoscelli

la serra

l'erba

la carrozzina

le verdure

il falò

il tubo di gomma

9

Il laboratorio

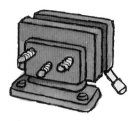

la morsa

la carta vetrata

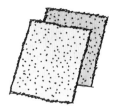

il trapano

la scala

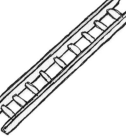

la sega

la segatura

il calendario

la cassetta
degli arnesi

le viti

il cacciavite

l'asse

i trucioli

il coltellino

10

le puntine

il ragno

i bulloni

i dadi

la ragnatela

la botte

la mosca

l'ascia

il metro

il martello

la lima

la vernice

la pialla

il legno

i chiodi

il piano di lavoro

i barattoli

11

La strada

il negozio

il buco

il bar

l'ambulanza

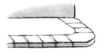

il marciapiede

la statua

il comignolo

il tetto

la scavatrice

l'albergo

l'autobus

l'uomo

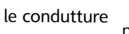

la macchina della polizia

le condutture

il martello pneumatico

la scuola

il campo giochi

il taxi

le strisce pedonali

la fabbrica

il camion

il semaforo

il cinema

il furgone

lo schiacciasassi

il rimorchio

la casa

il mercato

gli scalini

la motocicletta

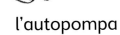
la bicicletta

l'autopompa

il vigile urbano

la macchina

la donna

il lampione

il palazzo

13

il trenino

i dadi

il flauto dolce

il robot

la collana

la macchina
fotografica

le perline

le bambole

la chitarra

l'anello

la casa
delle bambole

I giocattoli

l'armonica

il fischietto

le
costruzioni

il castello

il sottomarino

la tromba

le frecc

l'arco

il paracadute

la barca

i colori per
il viso

lo schiacciasassi

le maschere

la macchina
da corsa

il cavallo a dondolo

il salvadanaio

le biglie

le marionette

il pianoforte

gli astronauti

il razzo

la gru

le carte
da gioco

i tamburi

i soldatini

gli acquarelli

le altalene

la buca di sabbia

il picnic

l'aquilone

il gelato

il cane

il cancello

il sentiero

la rana

lo scivolo

Il parco

la panchina

i girini

il lago

i pattini in linea

il cespuglio

16

il bebè

lo skateboard

la terra

il passeggino

l'altalena
a bilico

i bambini

il triciclo

gli uccelli

la cancellata

la palla

la barca

lo spago

la pozzanghera

gli anatroccoli

la corda
per saltare

gli alberi

l'aiuola

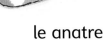
i cigni

il guinzaglio

le anatre

Gli animali

il panda

le ali

l'aquila

l'ippopotamo

il pipistrello

il gorilla

le zampe

il canguro

la scimmia

l'iceberg

il pinguino

la coda

il lupo

il coccodrillo

l'orso

le piume

il pellicano

lo struzzo

il delfino

il leone

i leoncini

la giraffa

il cervo

il dromedario

la foca

l'orso polare

la tartaruga

la proboscide

l'elefante

il rinoceronte

il bisonte

le corna

il castoro

la capra

la zebra

il serpente

lo squalo

la balena

la tigre

il leopardo

19

I trasporti

i binari

il locomotore

i respingenti

i vagoni

il macchinista

il treno merci

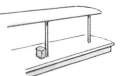

la pensilina

il controllore

la valigia

la biglietteria automatica

La stazione ferroviaria

La stazione di servizio

i segnali

lo zaino

i fari

il motore

la ruota

la batteria

20

l'aereo

l'elicottero

la pista di atterraggio

la torre di controllo

L'aeroporto

il personale di bordo

il pilota

l'autolavaggio

il portabagagli

la benzina

il carro attrezzi

AUTOLAVAGGIO

il distributore di benzina

l'autocisterna

la chiave inglese

lo pneumatico

il cofano

l'olio

21

il mulino a vento

la mongolfiera

la farfalla

la lucertola

le pietre

la volpe

il ruscello

il segnale
stradale

il riccio

La campagna

la montagna

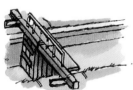

la chiusa

lo scoiattolo

la foresta

il tasso

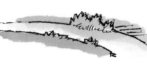

il fiume

la strada

22

le tende

il canale

i ceppi

il villaggio

la falena

il ponte

la chiatta

la cascata

il gufo

la galleria

i volpacchiotti

la talpa

il pescatore

i massi

il rospo

il treno

la roulotte

la collina

il mucchio di fieno

il cane pastore

gli agnelli

lo stagno

i pulcini

il fienile

il porcile

il toro

il pollaio

il trattore

La fattoria

il gallo

le oche

l'autocisterna

il capannone

il fango

il carretto

24

l'agricoltore

il campo

le galline

il vitello

la staccionata

la sella

la stalla

la mucca

l'aratro

il frutteto

la scuderia

i maialini

l'asino

i tacchini

lo spaventapasseri

la casa colonica

il fieno

le pecore

le balle di paglia

il cavallo

i maiali

25

Al mare

la barca a vela

il mare

il remo

il faro

la paletta

il secchiello

la stella marina

il castello di sabbia

l'ombrellone

la bandiera

il marinaio

la conchiglia

il granchio

il gabbiano

l'isola

il motoscafo

lo sci nautico

le onde

il cappello
da sole

la scogliera

la nave

la canoa

la fune

i ciottoli

le alghe

la rete

la pagaia

il peschereccio

le pinne

la crema solare

il pesce

il costume
da bagno

la petroliera

la spiaggia

la barca a remi

la sedia a sdraio

le forbici

$$2 + 2 = 4$$
$$2 + 3 = 5$$

le addizioni

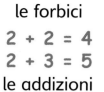

la gomma

il righello

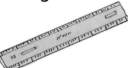

le fotografie

i pennarelli

la creta

i colori

il bambino

la matita

il banco

A scuola

la lavagna

i libri

la penna

la colla

i gessetti

il disegno

il cestino della carta

l'insegnante

la scatola

la carta geografica

il pennello

il soffitto

la parete

il pavimento

il quaderno

a b c d e f
g h i j k l m
n o p q r s t
u v w x y z

l'alfabeto

la spilla

l'acquario

la carta

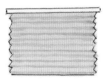

l'avvolgibile

il cavalletto

a b c d e f
g h i j k l m
n o p q r s t
u v w x y z

2 + 2 = 4
2 + 3 = 5

la maniglia della porta

la pianta

il mappamondo

la bambina

i pastelli

la lampada

l'infermiere

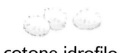

il cotone idrofilo

la medicina

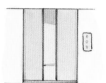

l'ascensore

la vestaglia

le grucce

le pillole

il vassoio

l'orologio

il termometro

la tenda

L'ospedale

la mela

il gesso

la fascia

la sedia
a rotelle

il puzzle

la dottoressa

la siringa

Dal dottore

le pantofole

il computer

il cerotto

la banana

l'uva

il cestino

i giocattoli

la pera

le cartoline

il pannolino

il bastone

il guanciale

la camicia
da notte

il pigiama

l'arancia

i fazzoletti
di carta

il fumetto

la sala
d'aspetto

La festa

il palloncino

i regali

la cioccolata

gli occhiali

la caramella

la finestra

i fuochi d'artificio

il nastro

la torta

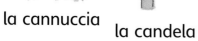

la cannuccia

la candela

le decorazioni di carta

i giocattoli

il mandarino

il salame

l'orsacchiotto

la salsiccia

le patatine

i costumi

la ciliegia

il succo di frutta

il lampone

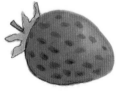

la fragola

la lampadina

il panino

il burro

il biscotto

il formaggio

il pane

la tovaglia

33

Il negozio

il pompelmo

la carota

il cavolfiore

il porro

il fungo

il cetriolo

il limone

il sedano

l'albicocca

il melone

la
borsa della spesa

formaggi

frutta e verdura

la cipolla

il cavolo

la pesca

la lattuga

i piselli

il pomodoro

34

le uova

 la susina

 la farina

la bilancia

i barattoli

 la carne

 l'ananas

 lo yogurt

 il cestino

 le bottiglie

 la borsa

 il borsellino

 i soldi

 il cibo in scatola

 il carrello

 le patate

 gli spinaci

 i fagiolini

 la cassa

la zucca

I pasti

la colazione

l'uovo sodo

il pranzo

il pane tostato

la marmellata

il caffè

l'uovo fritto

i cereali

la cioccolata calda

la panna

il latte

il miele

il sale

il pepe

lo zucchero

il tè

la teiera

le frittelle

i panini

36

la cena

il prosciutto

la minestra

la frittata

le bacchette

l'insalata

l'hamburger

il pollo

il riso

il ketchup

gli spaghetti

il purè

la pizza

le patatine fritte

i dolci

37

Io

la testa

i capelli

il viso

le sopracciglia

l'occhio

il naso

la guancia

la bocca

le labbra

il braccio

il gomito

la pancia

i denti

la lingua

il mento

le orecchie

il collo

le spalle

le dita dei piedi

il piede

la gamba

il ginocchio

il torace

la schiena

il sedere

la mano

il pollice

le dita della mano

I vestiti

i calzini

le mutande

la canottiera

i pantaloni

i jeans

la maglietta

la gonna

la camicia

la cravatta

i pantaloncini

la calzamaglia

il vestito

il maglione

la felpa

il cardigan

la sciarpa

il fazzoletto

le scarpe da ginnastica

le scarpe

i sandali

gli stivali di gomma

i guanti

le tasche

la cintura

la fibbia

la cerniera lampo

i lacci per le scarpe

i bottoni

le asole

il cappotto

il giubbotto

il berretto

il cappello

39

I mestieri

l'attore   l'attrice

il cuoco

i cantanti

i ballerini

il macellaio

i poliziotti

l'astronauta

il falegname

il pompiere

l'artista

il giudice

i meccanici

il parrucchiere

la camionista

il conducente
di autobus

il cameriere   la cameriera

il postino

la dentista

il subacqueo

l'imbianchino

la fornaia

La famiglia

il figlio
il fratello

la figlia
la sorella

la madre
la moglie

il padre
il marito

la zia   lo zio

l'animale
domestico

il cugino

il nonno

la nonna

41

Le azioni

sorridere

piangere

pensare

ascoltare

ridere

acchiappare

lanciare

rompere

dipingere

scrivere

spaccare

tagliare

mangiare

parlare

scavare

portare

bere

fare

saltare

ballare

lavarsi

lavorare
a maglia

camminare carponi

giocare

guardare

arrampicarsi

fare a botte

dormire

prendere

saltare con
la corda

cucire

aspettare

cucinare

nascondersi

leggere

comprare

spingere

cantare

soffiare

tirare

spazzare

raccogliere

cadere

camminare

correre

stare seduti

43

I contrari

lontano

vicino

buono

cattivo

in cima

in fondo

freddo

caldo

bagnato

asciutto

sporco

pulito

sopra

sotto

grasso

magro

aperto

chiuso

piccolo

grande

pochi

molti

primo

ultimo

sinistra

fuori

dentro

facile

difficile

vuoto

pieno

morbido

duro

davanti

alto

lento

veloce

dietro

basso

lungo

corto

morto

vivo

scuro

chiaro

su

vecchio

destra

nuovo

giù

45

I giorni

lunedì

martedì

mercoledì

giovedì

venerdì

sabato

domenica

il calendario

la mattina

il sole

la sera

la luna

la stella

la notte

lo Spazio

il pianeta

l'astronave

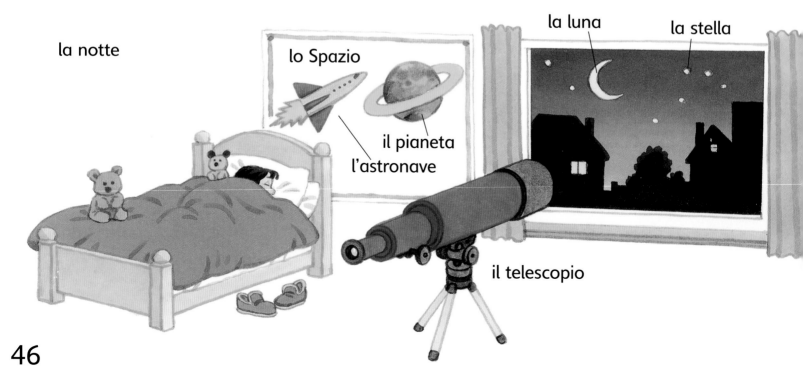

il telescopio

I giorni speciali

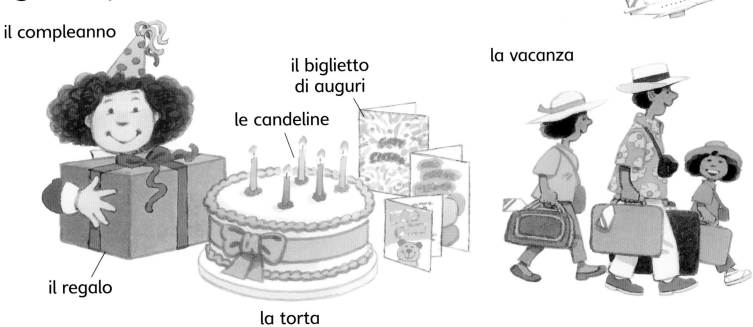

il compleanno

il biglietto di auguri

le candeline

la vacanza

il regalo

la torta

il matrimonio

gli ospiti

la macchina fotografica

la damigella d'onore

la sposa

lo sposo

il fotografo

Natale

la renna

la slitta

Babbo Natale

l'albero di Natale

47

Il tempo

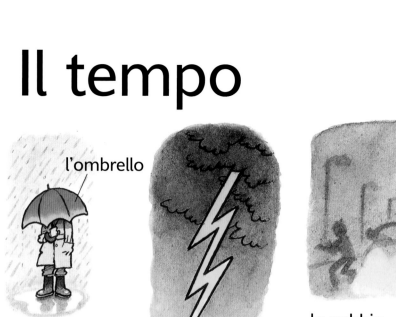

l'ombrello

la pioggia

il lampo

la nebbia

il sole

le nuvole

il cielo

la neve

la rugiada

il vento

la foschia

la brina

l'arcobaleno

Le stagioni

la primavera

l'estate

l'autunno

l'inverno

Gli animali domestici

il criceto

il veterinario

la cuccia

il porcellino d'India

il cagnolino

il cane

il pappagallino

il pappagallo

il cibo

il becco

il canarino

la gabbia

il coniglio

il gatto

la cesta

il gattino

il topolino

il latte

i pesci rossi

49

Lo sport

la vela

il canottaggio

lo snowboard

la vela

il windsurf

la pallacanestro

la racchetta

il cricket

il karatè

la mazza

il tennis

il football americano

la ginnastica artistica

la palla

il baseball

la danza

la canna da pesca

l'esca

la pesca

il rugby

i tuffi

la piscina

il nuoto

la corsa campestre

il tiro con l'arco

il bersaglio

il volo libero

il jogging

il casco

il ciclismo

l'alpinismo

il judo

il cavallo

il pony

l'armadietto

il calcio

l'equitazione

lo spogliatoio

il badminton

il ping-pong

i pattini

il pattinaggio su ghiaccio

i bastoncini da sci

la seggiovia

gli sci

lo sci

il sumo

51

I colori

arancione

verde

nero

grigio

rosso

marrone

rosa

bianco

blu

viola

giallo

Le forme

il rombo

il cono

il rettangolo

il cerchio

la stella

il cubo

l'ovale

il triangolo

il quadrato

la falce di luna

52

I numeri

1	uno	
2	due	
3	tre	
4	quattro	
5	cinque	
6	sei	
7	sette	
8	otto	
9	nove	
10	dieci	
11	undici	
12	dodici	
13	tredici	
14	quattordici	
15	quindici	
16	sedici	
17	diciassette	
18	diciotto	
19	diciannove	
20	venti	

Il luna park

la giostra

lo zucchero filato

la ruota

il trenino dei fantasmi

il pop-corn

il tappetino

lo scivolo

l'autoscontro

il lancio del cerchio

le montagne russe

Il circo

il funambolo

l'asta

il trapezio

camminare
sulla corda

l'equilibrista

la scala
di corda

la rete di
sicurezza

gli acrobati

il coniglio

il domatore

il cane

il cerchio

il cilindro

il giocoliere

il farfallino

l'orchestra

la cavallerizza

il pagliaccio

Word list

In this list, you can find all the Italian words in this book in alphabetical order. Next to each one, you can see its pronunciation (how to say it) in italics (*like this*), and then its English translation.

Remember that Italian nouns (words for things) are either masculine or feminine (see page 3). In the list, each one has **il**, **lo**, **la**, **l'**, **i**, **gli** or **le** in front of it. These all mean "the". The words with **il** or **lo** are masculine, those with **la** are feminine. Italian nouns that begin with "a", "e", "i", "o" or "u" have **l'** in front of them. After the word you will see (m) or (f) to show whether it is masculine or feminine.

Plural nouns (a noun is a plural if you are talking about more than one, for example "cats") have **i** or **gli** in front if they are masculine, or **le** if they are feminine.

About Italian pronunciation
Read the pronunciation as if it were an English word, but try to remember the following points about how Italian words are said:

All the letters in an Italian word are sounded, except **h**. Double letters, like **ll** or **nn**, sound a little longer than usual.

c before **e** or **i** is pronounced **ch**;
ch before **e** or **i** is pronounced **k**;
gh before **e** or **i** is pronounced **g** as in **get**;
sc before **e** or **i** is pronounced **sh**;
z is pronounced **ts**.

Most Italian words have a part that you stress, or say louder (like the "day" part of the English word "today"). The part of the word that you should stress is shown in bold italics (***like this***) in the pronunciation guide.

In the guide, ***ay*** is like the ***a*** in "date";
o is always like the ***o*** in "hot";
ow is always like the ***ow*** in "cow";
g is always like the ***g*** in "get";
ly is like the ***lli*** in "million";
ny is like the ***ni*** in "onion";
ye is always like the ***ye*** in "yet".

A

acchiappare	*akkyap**par**ay*	to catch
l'acqua (f)	***lak**wa*	water
gli acquarelli	*lyee akwa**rel**lee*	paints
l'acquario (m)	*lak**war**yo*	aquarium
gli acrobati	*lyee a**krob**atee*	acrobats
le addizioni	*lay addee**tsyo**nee*	sums
l'aereo (m)	*la-**ay**rayo*	plane
l'aeroporto	*la-ayro**por**to*	airport
gli agnelli	*lyee a**nyel**lee*	lambs
l'agricoltore	*lagreekol**tor**ay*	farmer
l'aiuola (f)	*la-**yuol**a*	flower bed
l'albergo (m)	*lal**bair**go*	hotel
gli alberi	*lyee **al**bairee*	trees
l'albero (m)	***lal**bairo*	tree
l'albero (m) di Natale	***lal**bairo dee na**tal**ay*	Christmas tree
l'albicocca (f)	*lalbee**kok**ka*	apricot
l'alfabeto (m)	*lalfa**bay**to*	alphabet
le alghe	*lay **al**gay*	seaweed
le ali	*lay **al**ee*	wings
l'alpinismo (m)	*lalpee**neez**mo*	climbing
l'altalena (f) a bilico	*lalta**lay**na a **bee**leeko*	seesaw
le altalene	*lay alta**lay**nay*	swings
alto	***al**to*	high
l'alveare (m)	*lalvay**ar**ay*	beehive
l'ambulanza (f)	*lamboo**lan**tsa*	ambulance
l'ananas (m)	***la**nanass*	pineapple
le anatre	*lay **a**natray*	ducks
gli anatroccoli	*lyee ana**trok**kolee*	ducklings
l'anello (m)	*la**nel**lo*	ring
l'animale domestico (m)	*lanee**mal**ay do**mes**teeko*	pet
gli animali	*lyee anee**mal**ee*	animals
gli animali domestici	*lyee anee**mal**ee do**mes**teechee*	pets
l'annaffiatoio (m)	*lanaffya**toy**o*	watering can
l'annaffiatore (m)	*lanaffya**tor**ay*	sprinkler
l'ape (f)	***la**pay*	bee
aperto	*a**pair**to*	open
l'aquila (f)	***lak**weela*	eagle
l'aquilone (m)	*lakwee**lo**nay*	kite
l'arancia (f)	*la**ran**cha*	orange (fruit)
arancione	*aran**cho**nay*	orange (colour)
l'aratro (m)	*la**ra**tro*	plough
l'arco (m)	***lar**ko*	bow (and arrows)
l'arcobaleno (m)	*larkoba**lay**no*	rainbow
l'armadietto (m)	*larma**dyet**to*	cupboard
l'armadio (m)	*lar**mad**yo*	wardrobe
l'armonica (f)	*lar**mo**neeka*	mouth organ
arrampicarsi	*arrampee**kar**see*	to climb
l'artista (m/f)	*lar**tees**ta*	artist
l'ascensore (m)	*lashen**sor**ay*	lift
l'ascia (f)	***la**sha*	axe
l'asciugamano (m)	*lashooga**ma**no*	towel
asciutto	*a**shoot**to*	dry
ascoltare	*askol**tar**ay*	to listen
l'asino (m)	***la**zeeno*	donkey
le asole	*lay **a**zolay*	button holes
aspettare	*aspet**tar**ay*	to wait
l'aspirapolvere (m)	*laspeera**pol**vairay*	vacuum cleaner
l'asse (f)	***las**say*	plank
l'asse (f) da stiro	***las**say da **stee**ro*	board
l'asta (f)	***las**ta*	pole
l'astronave (f)	*lastro**na**vay*	spaceship
l'astronauta (m)	*lastro**now**ta*	astronaut
gli astronauti	*lyee astro**now**tee*	astronauts, spacemen
l'attaccapanni (m)	*lattakka**pan**nee*	pegs
l'attore (m)	*lat**tor**ay*	actor
l'attrice (f)	*lat**tree**chay*	actress
l'autobus (m)	***low**toboos*	bus
l'autocisterna (f)	*lowtochees**tair**na*	tanker lorry
l'autolavaggio (m)	*lowtola**vaj**jo*	car wash
l'autopompa (f)	*lowto**pom**pa*	fire engine
l'autoscontro (m)	*lowto**skon**tro*	dodgems
l'autunno (m)	*low**toon**no*	autumn

l'avvolgibile (m)	lavvol**jee**beelay	blind
le azioni	lay a**tsyo**nee	actions

B

Babbo Natale	**bab**bo na**ta**lay	Father Christmas
le bacchette	lay bak**ket**tay	chopsticks
il badminton	eel **bad**meenton	badminton
bagnato	ba**nya**to	wet
il bagno	eel **ban**yo	bathroom
la balena	la ba**lay**na	whale
ballare	bal**la**ray	to dance
le balle di paglia	lay **bal**lay dee **pal**ya	straw bales
i ballerini	ee ballai**ree**nee	dancers
la bambina	la bam**bee**na	girl
i bambini	ee bam**bee**nee	children
il bambino	eel bam**bee**no	boy
le bambole	lay **bam**bolay	dolls
la banana	la ba**na**na	banana
il banco	eel **ban**ko	desk
la bandiera	la ban**dyai**ra	flag
il bar	eel **bar**	café
i barattoli	ee ba**rat**tolee	pots, jars
la barca	la **bar**ka	boat
la barca a vela	la **bar**ka a **vay**la	sailing boat
la barca a remi	la **bar**ka a **ray**mee	rowing boat
il baseball	eel **bayz**bol	baseball
basso	**bas**so	low
il bastone	eel bas**to**nay	stick
i bastoncini da sci	ee baston**chee**nee da shee	ski poles
la batteria	la battai**ree**a	battery
il bebè	eel be**bay**	baby
il becco	eel **bek**ko	beak
la benzina	la ben**tsee**na	petrol
bere	**bair**ay	to drink
il berretto	eel bair**ret**to	cap
il bersaglio	eel bair**sal**yo	target
bianco	**byan**ko	white
i bicchieri	ee beek**kyai**ree	glasses (for drinking)
la bicicletta	la beechee**klet**ta	bicycle
le biglie	lay **beel**yay	marbles
la biglietteria automatica	la beelyettai**ree**a owto**ma**teeka	ticket machine
il biglietto di auguri	eel beel**yet**to dee ow**goo**ree	birthday card
la bilancia	la beel**an**cha	scales
i binari	ee bee**na**ree	railway track
il biscotto	eel bees**kot**to	biscuit
il bisonte	eel bee**zon**tay	bison
blu	**bloo**	blue
la bocca	la **bok**ka	mouth
il bollitore	eel bollee**to**ray	kettle
la borsa	la **bor**sa	handbag
la borsa della spesa	la **bor**sa **del**la **spay**za	carrier bag
il borsellino	eel borsel**lee**no	wallet
la botte	la **bot**tay	barrel
le bottiglie	lay bot**teel**yay	bottles
i bottoni	ee bot**to**nee	buttons
il braccio	eel **bra**cho	arm
la brina	la **bree**na	frost
il bruco	eel **broo**ko	caterpillar

la buca di sabbia	la **boo**ka dee **sab**bya	sandpit
il buco	eel **boo**ko	hole
i bulloni	ee bool**lo**nee	bolts
buono	**bwo**no	good
il burro	eel **boor**ro	butter

C

il cacciavite	eel kacha**vee**tay	screwdriver
cadere	ka**dair**ay	to fall
il caffè	eel kaf**fay**	coffee
il cagnolino	eel kanyo**lee**no	puppy
il calcio	eel **kal**cho	football
caldo	**kal**do	hot
il calendario	eel kalen**dar**yo	calendar
la calzamaglia	la kaltsa**mal**ya	tights
i calzini	ee kalt**see**nee	socks
la camera da letto	la **kam**aira da **let**to	bedroom
la cameriera	la kamair**yai**ra	waitress
il cameriere	eel kamair**yai**ray	waiter
la camicia	la ka**mee**cha	shirt
la camicia da notte	la ka**mee**cha da **not**tay	nightdress
il camion	eel **kam**yon	lorry
il/la camionista	eel/la kamyo**nees**ta	lorry driver
camminare	kammee**na**ray	to walk
camminare carponi	kammee**na**ray kar**po**nee	to crawl
camminare sulla corda	kammee**na**ray **sool**la **kor**da	to walk a tightrope
la campagna	la kam**pan**ya	country
il campo	eel **kam**po	field
il campo giochi	eel **kam**po **jo**kee	playground
il canale	eel ka**na**lay	canal
il canarino	eel kana**ree**no	canary
la cancellata	la kanchel**la**ta	railings
il cancello	eel kan**chel**lo	gate
la candela	la kan**day**la	candle
le candeline	lay kande**lee**nay	cake candles
il cane	eel **ka**nay	dog
il cane pastore	eel **ka**nay pas**to**ray	sheepdog
il canguro	eel kan**goo**ro	kangaroo
la canna da pesca	la **kan**na da **pes**ka	fishing rod
la cannuccia	la kan**noo**cha	straw
la canoa	la ka**no**a	canoe
il canottaggio	eel kanot**taj**jo	rowing
la canottiera	la kanot**tyai**ra	vest
i cantanti	ee kan**tan**tee	singers
cantare	kan**ta**ray	to sing
il capannone	eel kapan**no**nay	barn
i capelli	ee ka**pel**lee	hair
il cappello	eel kap**pel**lo	hat
il cappello da sole	eel kap**pel**lo da **so**lay	sun hat
il cappotto	eel kap**pot**to	coat
la capra	la **kap**ra	goat
la caramella	la kara**mel**la	sweet
il cardigan	eel **kar**deegan	cardigan
la carne	la **kar**nay	meat
la carota	la ka**ro**ta	carrot
il carrello	eel kar**rel**lo	trolley
il carretto	eel kar**ret**to	cart
la carriola	la kar**ryo**la	wheelbarrow
il carro attrezzi	eel **kar**ro at**tret**tsee	breakdown lorry

la carrozzina	la karrott**see**na	pram
la carta	la **kar**ta	paper
la carta geografica	la **kar**ta jayo**gra**feeka	map
la carta igienica	la **kar**ta ee**je**neeka	toilet paper
la carta vetrata	la **kar**ta ve**tra**ta	sandpaper
le carte da gioco	lay **kar**tay da **jok**o	playing cards
le cartoline	lay karto**lee**nay	cards
la casa	la **ka**za	house
la casa colonica	la **ka**za ko**lo**neeka	farmhouse
la casa delle bambole	la **ka**za **del**lay **bam**bolay	dolls' house
la cascata	la kas**ka**ta	waterfall
il casco	eel **kas**ko	helmet
il casotto	eel ka**zot**to	shed
la cassa	la **kas**sa	checkout
la cassetta degli arnesi	la kas**set**ta **del**yee ar**nay**zee	tool box
il cassetto	eel kas**set**to	drawer
il cassettone	eel kas**set**tonay	chest of drawers
il castello	eel kas**tel**lo	castle
il castello di sabbia	eel kas**tel**lo dee **sab**bya	sandcastle
il castoro	eel kas**tor**o	beaver
cattivo	kat**tee**vo	bad
la cavallerizza	la kavallai**reet**tsa	bareback rider
il cavalletto	eel kaval**let**to	easel
il cavallo	eel ka**val**lo	horse
il cavallo a dondolo	eel ka**val**lo a **don**dolo	rocking horse
il cavolfiore	eel kavol**fyor**ay	cauliflower
il cavolo	eel **ka**volo	cabbage
la cena	la **chay**na	supper, dinner
i ceppi	ee **chep**pee	logs
il cerchio	eel **chair**kyo	circle, hoop
i cereali	ee chairay**a**lee	cereal
la cerniera lampo	la chair**nyai**ra **lam**po	zip
il cerotto	eel chair**ot**to	sticking plaster
il cervo	eel **chair**vo	deer
il cespuglio	eel ches**pool**yo	bush
la cesta	la **ches**ta	basket
il cestino	eel ches**tee**no	shopping basket
il cestino della carta	eel ches**tee**no **del**la **kar**ta	waste paper basket
il cetriolo	eel chetree**o**lo	cucumber
chiaro	**kyar**o	light
la chiatta	la **kyat**ta	barge
la chiave	la **kya**vay	key
la chiave inglese	la **kya**vay een**glay**zay	spanner
la chiocciola	la **kyo**chola	snail
i chiodi	ee **kyo**dee	nails
la chitarra	la kee**tar**ra	guitar
la chiusa	la **kyoo**za	lock (canal)
chiuso	**kyoo**zo	closed
il cibo in scatola	eel **chee**bo een **ska**tola	tinned food
il cibo	eel **chee**bo	food
il ciclismo	eel chee**kleez**mo	cycling
il cielo	eel **chay**lo	sky
i cigni	ee **chee**nyee	swans
la ciliegia	la chee**lye**ja	cherry
il cilindro	eel chee**leen**dro	top hat
il cinema	eel **chee**nayma	cinema
cinque	**cheen**quay	five
la cintura	la cheen**too**ra	belt
la cioccolata	la chokko**la**ta	chocolate
la cioccolata calda	la chokko**la**ta **kal**da	hot chocolate
i ciottoli	ee **chot**tolee	pebbles
la cipolla	la chee**pol**la	onion
il circo	eel **cheer**ko	circus
la coccinella	la kochee**nel**la	ladybird
il coccodrillo	eel kokko**dreel**lo	crocodile
la coda	la **ko**da	tail
il cofano	eel **ko**fano	bonnet
la colazione	la kola**tsyo**nay	breakfast
la colla	la **ko**la	glue
la collana	la kol**la**na	necklace
la collina	la kol**lee**na	hill
il collo	eel **kol**lo	neck
i colori	ee ko**lor**ee	colours, paints
i colori per il viso	ee ko**lor**ee pair eel **vee**zo	face paints
i coltelli	ee kol**tel**lee	knives
il coltellino	eel kol**tel**leeno	penknife
il comignolo	eel komee**nyo**lo	chimney
il compleanno	eel komplay**an**no	birthday
comprare	kompra**ray**	to buy
il computer	eel kom**pyoo**tair	computer
la conchiglia	la kon**kee**lya	shell
il conducente di autobus	eel kondoo**chen**tay dee **ow**toboos	bus driver
le condutture	lay kondoot**too**ray	pipes
il coniglio	eel ko**nee**lyo	rabbit
il cono	eel **ko**no	cone
i contrari	ee kon**trar**ee	opposites
il controllore	eel kontrol**lor**ay	ticket inspector
la corda per saltare	la **kor**da pair sal**tar**ay	skipping rope
le corna	lay **kor**na	horns
correre	**kor**rairay	to run
la corsa campestre	la **kor**sa kam**pes**tray	running race
corto	**kor**to	short
le costruzioni	lay kostroo**tsyo**nee	building blocks
il costume da bagno	eel kos**too**may da **ban**yo	swimsuit
i costumi	ee kos**too**mee	fancy dress
il cotone idrofilo	eel ko**to**nay ee**dro**feelo	cotton wool
la cravatta	la **kre**ma so**lar**ay	suncream
la crema solare	la kra**vat**ta	tie
la creta	la **kray**ta	clay
il criceto	la eel kree**chay**to	hamster
il cricket	eel **kree**ket	cricket
il cubo	eel **koo**bo	cube
i cucchiaini	ee kookkya-**ee**nee	teaspoons
la cuccia	la **koo**cha	kennel
la cucina	la koo**chee**na	kitchen
cucinare	koochee**nar**ay	to cook
cucire	koo**cheer**ay	to sew
il cugino	eel koo**jee**no	(male) cousin
la cugina	la koo**jee**na	(female) cousin
il cuoco	eel **kwo**ko	cook
il cuscino	eel koo**shee**no	cushion

D

i dadi (da officina)	ee **da**dee (da offee**chee**na)	nuts (workshop)
i dadi (per giocare)	ee **da**dee (pair jo**kar**ay)	dice
la damigella d'onore	la damee**jel**la do**nor**ay	bridesmaid
la danza	la **dan**tsa	dancing

davanti	da**van**tee	front
le decorazioni di carta	lay dekora**tsyo**nee dee **kar**ta	paper chains
il delfino	eel del**fee**no	dolphin
i denti	ee **den**tee	teeth
il dentifricio	eel dentee**free**cho	toothpaste
il/la dentista	eel/la den**tees**ta	dentist
dentro	**den**tro	inside
destra	**des**tra	right
il detersivo	eel detair**see**vo	washing powder
diciannove	deechan**no**vay	nineteen
diciassette	deechas**set**tay	seventeen
diciotto	dee**chot**to	eighteen
dieci	**dyech**ee	ten
dietro	**dyet**ro	behind
difficile	deef**fee**cheelay	difficult
dipingere	dee**peen**jairay	to paint
il disegno	eel dee**sen**yo	drawing
il distributore di benzina	eel deestreeboo**tor**ay dee ben**tsee**na	petrol pump
le dita dei piedi	lay **dee**ta day **pyed**ee	toes
le dita della mano	lay **dee**ta **del**la **ma**no	fingers
il divano	eel dee**va**no	sofa
la doccia	la **do**cha	shower
dodici	**do**deechee	twelve
i dolci	ee **dol**chee	pudding
il domatore	eel doma**tor**ay	ringmaster
domenica	do**me**neeka	Sunday
la donna	la **don**na	woman
dormire	dor**meer**ay	to sleep
il dottore	eel dot**tor**ay	doctor
la dottoressa	la dotto**res**sa	(woman) doctor
il dromedario	eel drome**dar**yo	camel
due	**doo**ay	two
duro	**doo**ro	hard
il DVD	eel dayvay**day**	DVD

E

l'elefante (m)	lele**fan**tay	elephant
l'elicottero (m)	lelee**kot**tairo	helicopter
l'equilibrista (m)	lekweelee**brees**ta	tightrope walker
l'equitazione (f)	lekweeta**tsyo**nay	riding
l'erba (f)	**lair**ba	grass
l'esca (f)	**les**ka	bait
l'estate (f)	le**sta**tay	summer

F

la fabbrica	la **fab**breeka	factory
facile	**fa**cheelay	easy
i fagiolini	ee fajo**lee**nee	beans
la falce di luna	la **fal**chay dee **loo**na	crescent
il falegname	eel fale**nya**may	carpenter
la falena	la fa**lay**na	moth
il falò	eel fa**lo**	bonfire
la famiglia	la fa**mee**lya	family
il fango	eel **fan**go	mud
fare	**far**ay	to make, to do
fare a botte	**far**ay a **bot**tay	to fight
la farfalla	la far**fal**la	butterfly
il farfallino	eel farfal**lee**no	bow tie
la farina	la fa**ree**na	flour
il faro	eel **fa**ro	lighthouse
i fari	ee **far**ee	headlights
la fascia	la **fa**sha	bandage
la fattoria	la fatto**ree**a	farm

i fazzoletti di carta	ee fatto**let**tee dee **kar**ta	tissues
il fazzoletto	eel fatto**let**to	handkerchief
la felpa	la **fel**pa	sweatshirt
il ferro da stiro	eel **fair**ro da **stee**ro	iron
la festa	la **fes**ta	party
i fiammiferi	ee fyam**mee**fairee	matches
la fibbia	la **feeb**bya	buckle
il fienile	eel fye**nee**lay	hay loft
il fieno	eel **fye**no	hay
la figlia	la **fee**lya	daughter
il figlio	eel **fee**lyo	son
la finestra	la fee**nes**tra	window
i fiori	ee **fyo**ree	flowers
il fischietto	eel fees**kyet**to	whistle
il fiume	eel **fyoo**may	river
il flauto dolce	eel **flow**to **dol**chay	recorder
la foca	la **fo**ka	seal
le foglie	lay **fo**lyay	leaves
il football americano	eel **foot**bol amairee**ka**no	American football
le forbici	lay **for**beechee	scissors
le forchette	lay for**ket**tay	forks
il forcone	eel for**ko**nay	garden fork
la foresta	la fo**res**ta	forest
il formaggio	eel for**maj**jo	cheese
le forme	lay **for**may	shapes
il fornaio	eel forna-**yo**	baker (man)
la fornaia	la forna-**ya**	baker (woman)
la foschia	la **fos**kya	mist
le fotografie	lay fotografa**fee**-ay	photos
il fotografo	eel fo**to**grafo	photographer
la fragola	la **fra**gola	strawberry
il fratello	eel fra**tel**lo	brother
le frecce	lay **fre**chay	arrows
freddo	**fred**do	cold
il frigorifero	eel freego**ree**fairo	fridge
la frittata	la freet**ta**ta	omelette
le frittelle	lay freet**tel**lay	pancakes
la frutta	la **froot**ta	fruit
il frutteto	eel fruit**tay**to	orchard
il fumetto	eel foo**met**to	comic
il fumo	eel **foo**mo	smoke
il funambolo	eel foo**nam**bolo	tightrope walker
la fune	la **foo**nay	rope
il fungo	eel **foon**go	mushroom
i fuochi d'artificio	ee **fwo**kee dartee**fee**cho	fireworks
fuori	**fwo**ree	outside
il furgone	eel foor**go**nay	van

G

la gabbia	la **gab**bya	cage
il gabbiano	eel gab**bya**no	seagull
il gabinetto	eel gabee**net**to	toilet
la galleria	la gallai**ree**a	tunnel
le galline	lay gal**lee**nay	hens
il gallo	eel **gal**lo	cockerel
la gamba	la **gam**ba	leg
il gattino	eel gat**tee**no	kitten
il gatto	eel **gat**to	cat
il gelato	eel je**la**to	ice cream
i gessetti	ee jes**set**tee	chalks
il gesso	eel **jes**so	plaster
giallo	**jal**lo	yellow
il giardino	eel jar**dee**no	garden
la ginnastica artistica	la jeen**nas**teeka ar**tees**teeka	gymnastics

il ginocchio	eel jee**nok**kyo	knee
giocare	jo**kar**ay	to play
i giocattoli	ee jo**kat**tolee	toys
il giocoliere	eel joko**lyair**ay	juggler
il giornale	eel jor**nal**ay	newspaper
i giorni	ee **jor**nee	days
i giorni speciali	ee **jor**nee spe**chal**ee	special days
la giostra	la **jo**stra	merry-go-round
giovedì	jove**dee**	Thursday
la giraffa	la jee**raff**a	giraffe
i girini	ee jee**ree**nee	tadpoles
giù	**joo**	down
il giubbotto	eel joob**botto**	waistcoat
il giudice	eel **joo**deechay	judge
il gomito	eel **go**meeto	elbow
la gomma	la **gom**ma	rubber
la gonna	la **gon**na	skirt
il gorilla	eel go**reel**la	gorilla
il granchio	eel **gran**kyo	crab
grande	**gran**day	big
grasso	**gras**so	fat
il grembiule	eel grem**byoo**lay	apron
grigio	**gree**jo	grey
la gru	la **groo**	crane
le grucce	lay **groo**chay	crutches
la guancia	la **gwan**cha	cheek
il guanciale	eel gwan**chal**ay	pillow
i guanti	ee **gwan**tee	gloves
guardare	gwar**dar**ay	to look
il guinzaglio	eel gween**tsal**yo	lead
il gufo	eel **goo**fo	owl

H

| l'hamburger (m) | **lam**boorgair | hamburger |

I

l'iceberg (m)	**lies**bairg	iceberg
l'imbianchino (m)	leembyan**kee**no	house painter
in cima	een **chee**ma	on top
in fondo	een **fon**do	at the bottom
l'infermiera (f)	leenfair**myair**a	nurse (woman)
l'infermiere (m)	leenfair**myair**ay	nurse (man)
l'ingresso (m)	leen**gres**so	hall
l'insalata (f)	leensa**lat**a	salad
l'insegnante (m/f)	leense**nyan**tay	teacher
l'interruttore (m)	leentairroot**tor**ay	switch
l'inverno (m)	leen**vair**no	winter
io	**ee**o	me
l'ippopotamo (m)	leeppo**pot**amo	hippopotamus
l'isola (f)	**lee**zola	island

J

i jeans	ee **jeens**	jeans
il jogging	eel **jog**geeng	jogging
il judo	eel **joo**do	judo

K

| il karatè | eel kara**tay** | karate |
| il ketchup | eel **ke**chap | ketchup |

L

le labbra	lay **labb**ra	lips
il laboratorio	eel labora**tor**yo	workshop
i lacci per le scarpe	ee **la**chee pair lay **skar**pay	shoelaces
il lago	eel **la**go	lake
la lampada	la **lam**pada	lamp

la lampadina	la lampa**dee**na	light bulb
il lampione	eel lam**pyo**nay	street lamp
il lampo	eel **lam**po	lightning
il lampone	eel lam**po**nay	raspberry
lanciare	lan**char**ay	to throw
il lancio del cerchio	eel **lan**cho al **chair**kyo	hoop-la
il latte	eel **lat**tay	milk
la lattuga	la lat**too**ga	lettuce
la lavagna	la la**van**ya	board
il lavandino	eel lavan**dee**no	basin
lavarsi	la**var**see	to wash
la lavatrice	la lava**tree**chay	washing machine
il lavello	eel la**vel**lo	sink
lavorare a maglia	lavo**rar**ay a **mal**ya	to knit
leggere	**lej**jairay	to read
il legno	eel **len**yo	wood
lento	**len**to	slow
il lenzuolo	eel lent**swo**lo	sheet
i leoncini	ee layon**chee**nee	lion cubs
il leone	eel lay**o**nay	lion
il leopardo	eel layo**par**do	leopard
le lettere	lay **let**tairay	letters
il letto	eel **let**to	bed
i libri	ee **lee**bree	books
la lima	la **lee**ma	file
il limone	eel **lee**monay	lemon
la lingua	la **leen**gwa	tongue
il locomotore	eel lokomo**tor**ay	engine (train)
lontano	lon**tan**o	far
la lucertola	la loo**chair**tola	lizard
la luna	la **loo**na	moon
il luna park	eel **loo**na park	funfair
lunedì	loonay**dee**	Monday
lungo	**loon**go	long
il lupo	eel **loo**po	wolf

M

la macchina	la **mak**keena	car
la macchina da corsa	la **mak**keena da **kor**sa	racing car
la macchina della polizia	la **mak**keena **del**la polee**tsee**a	police car
la macchina fotografica	la **mak**keena fotogra**feek**a	camera
il macchinista	eel makkee**nees**ta	train driver
il macellaio	eel machel**la**-yo	butcher
la madre	la **ma**dray	mother
la maglietta	la mal**yet**ta	tee-shirt
il maglione	eel mal**yo**nay	pull-over
magro	**ma**gro	thin
i maiali	ee ma-**ya**lee	pigs
i maialini	ee ma-ya**lee**nee	piglets
il mandarino	eel manda**ree**no	clementine
mangiare	man**jar**ay	to eat
la maniglia della porta	la ma**neel**ya **del**la **por**ta	door handle
la mano	la **ma**no	hand
il mappamondo	eel mappa**mon**do	globe
il marciapiede	eel marcha**pyed**ay	pavement
il mare	eel **mar**ay	sea
il marinaio	eel mareena-yo	sailor
le marionette	lay maryo**net**tay	puppets
il marito	eel ma**ree**to	husband
la marmellata	la marmel**la**ta	jam
marrone	mar**ro**nay	brown
martedì	marte**dee**	Tuesday
il martello	eel mar**tel**lo	hammer

60

il martello pneumatico	eel martello pnayoomateeko	road drill
le maschere	lay maskairay	masks
i massi	ee massee	rocks
la matita	la mateeta	pencil
il matrimonio	eel matreemonyo	wedding
la mattina	la matteena	morning
le mattonelle	lay mattonellay	tiles
i mattoni	ee mattonee	bricks
la mazza	la mattsa	bat (sports)
i meccanici	ee mekkaneechee	mechanics
la medicina	la medeecheena	medicine
la mela	la mayla	apple
il melone	eel maylonay	melon
il mento	eel mento	chin
il mercato	eel mairkato	market
mercoledì	mairkolaydee	Wednesday
i mestieri	ee mestyairee	jobs
i mestoli	ee mestolee	wooden spoons
il metro	eel metro	tape measure
il miele	eel myelay	honey
la minestra	la meenestra	soup
la moglie	la molyay	wife
molti	moltee	many
la mongolfiera	la mongolfyaira	hot air balloon
la montagna	la montanya	mountain
le montagne russe	lay montanyay roossay	rollercoaster
la moquette	la mokett	fitted carpet
morbido	morbeedo	soft
la morsa	la morsa	vice
morto	morto	dead
la mosca	la moska	fly
la motocicletta	la motocheekletta	motorbike
il motore	eel motoray	engine (car)
il motoscafo	eel motoskafo	motor boat
la mucca	la mookka	cow
il mucchio di fieno	eel mookkyo dee fyeno	haystack
il mulino a vento	eel mooleeno a vento	windmill
le mutande	lay mootanday	underpants

N

nascondersi	naskondairsee	to hide
il naso	eel nazo	nose
il nastro	eel nastro	ribbon
Natale	natalay	Christmas
la nave	la navay	ship
la nebbia	la nebbya	fog
il negozio	eel negotsyo	shop
nero	nairo	black
la neve	la nayvay	snow
il nido	eel needo	nest
la nonna	la nonna	grandmother
il nonno	eel nonno	grandfather
la notte	la nottay	night
nove	novay	nine
i numeri	ee noomairee	numbers
il nuoto	eel nwoto	swimming
nuovo	nwovo	new
le nuvole	lay noovolay	clouds

O

gli occhiali	lyee okeealee	glasses (to wear)
l'occhio (m)	lokkyo	eye
le oche	lay okay	geese
l'olio (m)	lolyo	oil
l'ombrello (m)	lombrello	umbrella
l'ombrellone (m)	lombrellonay	beach umbrella
le onde	lay onday	waves
l'orchestra (f)	lorkestra	orchestra
le orecchie	lay orekkyay	ears
l'orologio (m)	lorolojo	clock, watch
l'orsacchiotto (m)	lorsakkyotto	teddy bear
l'orso (m)	lorso	bear
l'orso (m) polare	lorso polaray	polar bear
l'ospedale (m)	lospedalay	hospital
gli ospiti	lyee osspeetee	guests
l'osso (m)	losso	bone
otto	otto	eight
l'ovale (m)	lovalay	oval

P

la padella	la padella	frying pan
il padre	eel padray	father
la pagaia	la paga-ya	paddle
il pagliaccio	eel palyacho	clown
il palazzo	eel palattso	block of flats, building
la paletta (da giardino)	la paletta (da jardeeno)	trowel
la paletta (da spiaggia)	la paletta (da spyajja)	beach spade
la paletta (per la spazzatura)	la paletta (pair la spattsatoora)	dustpan
la palla	la palla	ball
la pallacanestro	la pallakanestro	basketball
il palloncino	eel palloncheeno	balloon
la panchina	la pankeena	bench
la pancia	la pancha	tummy
il panda	eel panda	panda
il pane	eel panay	bread
il pane tostato	eel panay tostato	toast
il panino	eel paneeno	sandwich
la panna	la panna	cream
il pannolino	eel pannoleeno	nappy
i pantaloncini	ee pantaloncheenee	shorts
i pantaloni	ee pantalonee	trousers
le pantofole	lay pantofolay	slippers
il pappagallino	eel pappagalleeno	budgerigar
il pappagallo	eel pappagallo	parrot
il paracadute	eel parakadootay	parachute
il parco	eel parko	park
la parete	la paraytay	wall
parlare	parlaray	to talk
il parrucchiere	eel parrookkyairay	hairdresser
il passeggino	eel passejjeeno	pushchair
i pastelli	ee pastellee	crayons
i pasti	ee pastee	meals
le patate	lay patatay	potatoes
le patatine	lay patateenay	crisps
le patatine fritte	lay patateenay freettay	chips
il pattinaggio su ghiaccio	eel patteenajjo soo gyacho	ice skating
i pattini	ee patteenee	skates
i pattini in linea	ee patteenee een leenaya	roller blades
la pattumiera	la pattoomyaira	rubbish bin
il pavimento	eel paveemento	floor
le pecore	lay paykoray	sheep
il pellicano	eel pelleekano	pelican
la penna	la penna	pen
i pennarelli	ee pennarellee	felt-tips
il pennello	eel pennello	paintbrush

61

pensare	*pensaray*	to think
la pensilina	*la penseeleena*	platform
le pentole	*le pentolay*	pans
il pepe	*eel paypay*	pepper
la pera	*la paira*	pear
le perline	*lay pairleenay*	beads
il personale di bordo	*eel pairsonalay dee bordo*	cabin crew
la pesca (frutta)	*la peska (frootta)*	peach
la pesca (attività)	*la peska (atteeveeta)*	fishing
il pescatore	*eel peskatoray*	fisherman
il pesce	*eel peshay*	fish
il peschereccio	*eel peskairecho*	fishing boat
i pesci rossi	*ee peshee rossee*	goldfish
la petroliera	*la petrolyaira*	oil tanker
il pettine	*eel petteenay*	comb
la pialla	*la pyalla*	(shaving) plane
il pianeta	*eel pyanayta*	planet
piangere	*pyanjairay*	to cry
il piano di lavoro	*eel pyano dee lavoro*	workbench
il pianoforte	*eel pyanofortay*	piano
la pianta	*la pyanta*	plant
i piatti	*ee pyattee*	plates
i piattini	*ee pyatteenee*	saucers
il piccione	*eel peechonay*	pigeon
piccolo	*peekkolo*	small
il picnic	*eel peekneek*	picnic
il piede	*eel pyeday*	foot
pieno	*pyeno*	full
le pietre	*lay pyetray*	stones
il pigiama	*eel peejama*	pyjamas
le pillole	*lay peellolay*	pills
il pilota	*eel peelota*	pilot
il ping-pong	*eel peeng-pong*	ping-pong
il pinguino	*eel peengweeno*	penguin
le pinne	*lay peennay*	flippers
la pioggia	*la pyojja*	rain
il pipistrello	*eel peepeestrello*	bat (animal)
la piscina	*la peesheena*	swimming pool
i piselli	*ee peezellee*	peas
la pista di atterraggio	*la peesta dee attairrajjo*	runway
le piume	*lay pyoomay*	feathers
il piumone	*eel pyoomonay*	duvet
la pizza	*la peettsa*	pizza
lo pneumatico	*lo pnayoomateeko*	tyre
pochi	*pokee*	few
i poliziotti	*ee poleetsyottee*	policemen
il pollaio	*eel polla-yo*	hen-house
il pollice	*eel polleechay*	thumb
il pollo	*eel pollo*	chicken
il pomodoro	*eel pomodoro*	tomato
il pompelmo	*eel pompelmo*	grapefruit
il pompiere	*eel pompyairay*	fireman
il ponte	*eel pontay*	bridge
il pony	*eel ponee*	pony
il pop-corn	*eel pop-korn*	popcorn
il porcellino d'India	*eel porchelleeno deendya*	guinea pig
il porcile	*eel porcheelay*	pigsty
il porro	*eel porro*	leek
la porta	*la porta*	door
il portabagagli	*eel portabagalyee*	boot (of car)
portare	*portaray*	to carry
i poster	*ee postair*	posters
il postino	*eel posteeno*	postman
la pozzanghera	*la pottsangaira*	puddle
il pranzo	*eel prantso*	lunch, dinner
prendere	*prendairay*	to take
la primavera	*la preemavaira*	spring
primo	*preemo*	first
la proboscide	*la probosheeday*	trunk
il prosciutto	*eel proshootto*	ham
i pulcini	*ee poolcheenee*	chickens
pulito	*pooleeto*	clean
le puntine	*lay poonteenay*	tacks
il purè	*eel pooray*	mashed potato
il puzzle	*eel pazol*	puzzle

Q

il quaderno	*eel kwadairno*	notebook
il quadrato	*eel kwadrato*	square
quattordici	*kwattordeechee*	fourteen
quattro	*kwattro*	four
quindici	*kweendeechee*	fifteen

R

la racchetta	*la rakketta*	racquet
raccogliere	*rakkolyairay*	to pick
il radiatore	*eel radyatoray*	radiator
la radio	*la radyo*	radio
la ragnatela	*la ranyatayla*	spider's web
il ragno	*eel ranyo*	spider
i ramoscelli	*ee ramoshellee*	twigs
la rana	*la rana*	frog
il rastrello	*eel rastrello*	rake
il razzo	*eel rattso*	rocket
il regalo	*eel regalo*	present
il remo	*eel remo*	oar
la renna	*la renna*	reindeer
i respingenti	*ee respeenjentee*	buffers
la rete	*la raytay*	net
la rete di sicurezza	*la raytay dee seekoorettsa*	safety net
il rettangolo	*eel rettangolo*	rectangle
il riccio	*eel reecho*	hedgehog
ridere	*reedairay*	to laugh
il righello	*eel reegello*	ruler
il rimorchio	*eel reemorkyo*	trailer
il rinoceronte	*eel reenochairontay*	rhinoceros
il riso	*eel reezo*	rice
il robot	*eel robot*	robot
il rombo	*eel rombo*	diamond (shape)
rompere	*rompairay*	to break
rosa	*roza*	pink
il rospo	*eel rospo*	toad
rosso	*rosso*	red
la roulotte	*la roolott*	caravan
il rubinetto	*eel roobeenetto*	tap
il rugby	*eel ragbee*	rugby
la rugiada	*la roojada*	dew
la ruota	*la rwota*	wheel, big wheel
il ruscello	*eel rooshello*	stream

S

sabato	*sabato*	Saturday
la sala d'aspetto	*la sala daspetto*	waiting room
il salame	*eel salamay*	salami
il sale	*eel salay*	salt
la salsiccia	*la salseecha*	sausage
saltare	*saltaray*	to jump
saltare con la corda	*saltaray con la korda*	to skip
il salvadanaio	*eel salvadana-yo*	money box

i sandali	ee *sandalee*	sandals
il sapone	eel *sapo*nay	soap
la scala	la *ska*la	ladder
la scala di corda	la *ska*la dee *kor*da	rope ladder
le scale	lay *ska*lay	stairs
gli scalini	lyee ska*lee*nee	steps
le scarpe	lay *skar*pay	shoes
le scarpe da ginnastica	lay *skar*pay da jeen*na*steeka	trainers
la scatola	la *ska*tola	box
scavare	ska*va*ray	to dig
la scavatrice	la skava*tree*chay	bulldozer
lo schiacciasassi	lo skyacha*sas*see	roller
la schiena	la *skye*na	back
gli sci	lyee *shee*	skis
lo sci	lo *shee*	skiing
lo sci nautico	lo shee *now*teeko	waterskiing
la sciarpa	la *shar*pa	scarf
la scimmia	la *sheem*mya	monkey
lo scivolo	lo *shee*volo	slide, helter-skelter
le scodelle	lay sko*del*lay	bowls
la scogliera	la sko*lyai*ra	cliff
lo scoiattolo	lo sko*yat*tolo	squirrel
la scopa	la *sko*pa	broom
scrivere	*skree*vairay	to write
la scuderia	la skoodai*ree*a	stable
la scuola	la *skwo*la	school
scuro	*skoo*ro	dark
il secchiello	eel sek*kyel*lo	bucket
il sedano	eel *say*dano	celery
il sedere	eel se*dai*ray	bottom
la sedia	la *say*dya	chair
la sedia a rotelle	la *say*dya a ro*tel*lay	wheelchair
la sedia a sdraio	la *say*dya a *zdra*-yo	deckchair
sedici	*say*deechee	sixteen
la sega	la *say*ga	saw
la segatura	la sayga*too*ra	sawdust
la seggiovia	la sejjo*vee*a	chairlift
il segnale stradale	eel sen*ya*lay *stra*dalay	signpost
i segnali	ee sen*ya*lee	signals
sei	*say*ee	six
la sella	la *sel*la	saddle
il semaforo	eel *se*maforo	traffic lights
i semi	ee *say*mee	seeds
il sentiero	eel sen*tyai*ro	path
la sera	la *sai*ra	evening
il serpente	eel sair*pen*tay	snake
la serra	la *sair*ra	greenhouse
sette	*set*tay	seven
lo sgabello	lo zga*bel*lo	stool
la siepe	la *sye*pay	hedge
sinistra	see*nee*stra	left
la siringa	la see*reen*ga	syringe
lo skateboard	lo *skayt*bord	skateboard
la slitta	la *sleet*ta	sleigh
lo snowboard	lo *sno*bord	snowboard
soffiare	sof*fya*ray	to blow
il soffitto	eel sof*feet*to	ceiling
il soggiorno	eel soj*jor*no	living room
i soldatini	ee solda*tee*nee	toy soldiers
i soldi	ee *sol*dee	money
il sole	eel *so*lay	sun
sopra	*so*pra	above
le sopracciglia	lay sopra*chee*lya	eyebrows
la sorella	la so*rel*la	sister
sorridere	sor*ree*dairay	to smile
sotto	*sot*to	below
il sottomarino	eel sottoma*ree*no	submarine
spaccare	spak*ka*ray	to chop
gli spaghetti	lyee spa*get*tee	spaghetti
lo spago	lo *spa*go	string
le spalle	lay *spal*lay	shoulders
lo spaventapasseri	lo spaventa*pas*sairee	scarecrow
lo Spazio	lo *spa*tsyo	space
spazzare	spat*tsa*ray	to sweep
la spazzatura	la spattsa*too*ra	rubbish
la spazzola	la *spat*tsola	brush, hairbrush
lo spazzolino	lo spattso*lee*no	toothbrush
lo spazzolone	lo spattso*lo*nay	mop
lo specchio	lo *spek*kyo	mirror
la spiaggia	la *spyaj*ja	beach
la spilla	la *speel*la	badge
gli spinaci	lyee spee*na*chee	spinach
spingere	*speen*jairay	to push
lo spogliatoio	lo spolya*to*yo	changing room
sporco	*spor*ko	dirty
lo sport	lo sport	sport
la sposa	la *spo*za	bride
lo sposo	lo *spo*zo	bridegroom
la spugna	la *spoo*nya	sponge
lo squalo	lo *skwa*lo	shark
la staccionata	la stacho*na*ta	fence
le stagioni	lay sta*jo*nee	seasons
lo stagno	lo *stan*yo	pond
la stalla	la *stal*la	cowshed
stare seduti	*sta*ray se*doo*tee	to sit
la statua	la *sta*tooa	statue
la stazione di servizio	la stat*syo*nay dee sair*veet*syo	garage
la stazione ferroviaria	la stat*syo*nay fairro*vyar*ya	station
la stella	la *stel*la	star
la stella marina	la *stel*la ma*ree*na	starfish
gli stivali di gomma	lyee stee*va*lee dee *gom*ma	boots, wellies
lo straccio	lo *stra*cho	duster
la strada	la *stra*da	street
le strisce pedonali	lay *stree*shay pedo*na*lee	pedestrian crossing
lo strofinaccio (m)	lo strofee*na*cho	tea towel
lo struzzo	lo *stroot*tso	ostrich
su	*soo*	up
il subacqueo	eel soo*bak*kwayo	diver
il succo di frutta	eel *sook*ko dee *froot*ta	fruit juice
il sumo	eel *soo*mo	sumo wrestling
la susina	la soo*zee*na	plum

T

i tacchini	ee tak*kee*nee	turkeys
tagliare	ta*lya*ray	to cut
la talpa	la *tal*pa	mole
i tamburi	ee tam*boo*ree	drums
il tappetino	eel tappay*tee*no	rug
il tappeto	eel tap*pay*to	carpet
la tartaruga	la tarta*roo*ga	tortoise
le tasche	lay *tas*kay	pockets
il tasso	eel *tas*so	badger
il tavolino	eel tavo*lee*no	small table
il taxi	eel *tak*see	taxi
le tazze	lay *tat*tsay	cups
il tè	eel *tay*	tea
la teiera	la ta*yai*ra	teapot

il telefono	eel te**lef**ono	telephone
il telescopio	eel tele**skop**yo	telescope
il televisore	eel televee**zor**ay	television
il tempo	eel **temp**o	weather
la tenda	la **ten**da	curtain, tent
le tende	lay **ten**day	curtains, tent
il tennis	eel **ten**nees	tennis
il termometro	eel tair**mo**maytro	thermometer
la terra	la **tair**ra	earth
la testa	la **tes**ta	head
il tetto	eel **tet**to	roof
la tigre	la **tee**gray	tiger
tirare	tee**rar**ay	to pull
il tiro con l'arco	eel **tee**ro kon **lar**ko	archery
il topolino	eel topo**lee**no	mouse
il torace	eel to**rach**ay	chest
il toro	eel **tor**o	bull
la torre di controllo	la **tor**ray dee kon**trol**lo	control tower
la torta	la **tor**ta	cake, birthday cake
il tosaerba	eel toza-**air**ba	lawnmower
la tovaglia	la to**val**ya	tablecloth
il trapano	eel **trap**ano	drill
il trapezio	eel tra**pet**syo	trapeze
i trasporti	ee tra**sport**ee	transport
il trattore	eel trat**tor**ay	tractor
tre	**tray**	three
tredici	**tray**deechee	thirteen
il trenino	eel tray**nee**no	toy train
il trenino dei fantasmi	eel tray**nee**no day fan**taz**mee	ghost train
il treno	eel **tray**no	train
il treno merci	eel **tray**no **mair**chee	goods train
il triangolo	eel tree**an**golo	triangle
il triciclo	eel tree**cheek**lo	tricycle
la tromba	la **trom**ba	trumpet
i trucioli	ee **troo**chyolee	shavings
il tubo di gomma	eel **too**bo dee **gom**ma	hosepipe
i tuffi	ee **toof**fee	diving

U

gli uccelli	lyee oo**chel**lee	birds
ultimo	**ool**teemo	last
undici	**oon**deechee	eleven
uno	**oo**no	one
l'uomo (m)	**lwo**mo	man
le uova	lay **wo**va	eggs
l'uovo (m) fritto	**lwo**vo **freet**to	fried egg
l'uovo (m) sodo	**lwo**vo sodo	hard-boiled egg
l'uva	**loo**va	grapes

V

la vacanza	la va**kant**sa	holiday
i vagoni	ee va**gon**ee	carriages
la valigia	la va**lee**ja	suitcase
la vanga	la **van**ga	spade
la vasca	la **vas**ka	bath
il vassoio	eel vas**so**yo	tray
vecchio	**vek**kyo	old
la vela	la **vay**la	sailing, sail
veloce	vay**lo**chay	fast
venerdì	venair**dee**	Friday
venti	**ven**tee	twenty
il vento	eel **ven**to	wind
verde	**vair**day	green
le verdure	lay vair**door**ay	vegetables
il verme	eel **vair**may	worm
la vernice	la vair**nee**chay	paint
la vespa	la **ves**pa	wasp
la vestaglia	la ves**tal**ya	dressing gown
i vestiti	ee ves**tee**tee	clothes
il vestito	eel ves**tee**to	dress
il veterinario	eel vetairee**nar**yo	vet
vicino	vee**chee**no	near
il vigile urbano	eel **vee**jeelay oor**ban**o	policeman (traffic police)
il villaggio	eel veel**laj**jo	village
viola	**vee**ola	purple
il viso	eel **vee**zo	face
il vitello	eel vee**tel**lo	calf
le viti	lay **vee**tee	screws
vivo	**vee**vo	alive
il volo libero	eel **vo**lo **lee**bairo	hang gliding
i volpacchiotti	ee volpak**kyot**tee	fox cubs
la volpe	la **vol**pay	fox
vuoto	**vwo**to	empty

W

il windsurf	eel **ween**sairf	windsurfing

Y

lo yogurt	lo **yo**goort	yogurt

Z

lo zaino	lo **tsa**-eeno	backpack
le zampe	lay **tsam**pay	paws
la zappa	la **tsap**pa	hoe
la zebra	la **tse**bra	zebra
la zia	la **tsee**a	aunt
lo zio	lo **tsee**o	uncle
la zucca	la **tsook**ka	pumpkin
lo zucchero	lo **tsook**kairo	sugar
lo zucchero filato	lo **tsook**kairo fee**la**to	candy floss